To Work is Human, but Retirement is Divine

By Yvette Jean Silver

PINNACLE BOOKS KENSINGTON PUBLISHING CORP. http://www.pinnacle.com

PINNACLE BOOKS are published by

Kensington Publishing Corp.
850 Third Avenue
New York, NY 10022

Pinnacle and the P logo Reg U.S. Pat. & TM Off.

First Printing: August, 1997
10   9   8   7   6   5   4   3   2   1

Printed in the United States of America

For my brother Dan.

Thanks to my parents, Martin and Denise, for their humor and love. Special thanks to Lynn Seligman and Paul Dinas for their patience and support in making this second book possible.

THERE ONCE WAS A TIME...

BUT THE MORE YOU WORKED, THE MORE WORK THERE WAS.

EVEN WHEN YOU DIDN'T HAVE A JOB,

WORK MADE HOUSE CALLS.

BUT YOU ALWAYS GAVE IT YOUR ALL,

AND WENT THE EXTRA MILE.

OR TOO SMALL.

YOU SACRIFICED ...   AND ECONOMIZED ...

AND EARNED YOUR PIECE OF THE PIE.

THEN ONE DAY...

AND IT SEEMS LIKE EVERYONE YOUR AGE IS OUT HAVING FUN.

SO INSTEAD OF TRYING TO KEEP UP,

THOUGH YOU HATE TO ADMIT IT, YOUR CHILDREN ARE RIGHT,

YOU CAN QUIT ANYTIME YOU LIKE.

EVERYONE WILL CELEBRATE,

AND PRAISE YOU TO THE SKY.

THOUGH IT FEELS LIKE IT WAS ONLY YESTERDAY,

BECAUSE FROM NOW ON, YOUR TIME IS YOUR OWN.

AT FIRST...

THEN YOU PLUNGE RIGHT IN.

SEEING YOUR KIDS:

BEFORE

AFTER

HOW YOU LOOK:

BEFORE

AFTER

THE ESSENTIALS:

BEFORE

AFTER

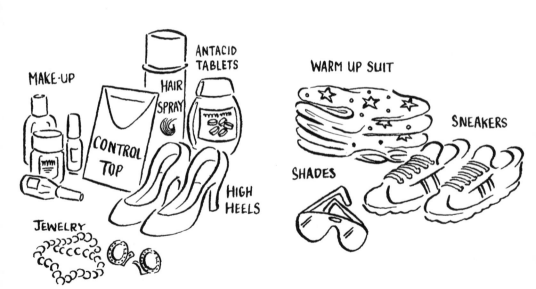

YOUR MORNINGS:

YOUR EVENINGS:

YOUR ENTIRE ROUTINE.

THERE'S SO MUCH TO DISCOVER...

AND DREAMS COME TRUE.

YOU HAVE ALL THE TIME IN THE WORLD...

TO FINISH THE THINGS YOU START,

AND START THINGS YOU WERE NEVER ABLE TO FINISH.

TO HOLD SOMEONE CLOSE,

AND REMEMBER PAST GLORIES.

BUT RETIREMENT IS DIVINE.